Then and Now

PEARSON

Scott
Foresman

Glenview, Illinois • Boston, Massachusetts • Mesa, Arizona
Shoreview, Minnesota • Upper Saddle River, New Jersey

ISBN-13: 978-0-328-38515-7
ISBN-10: 0-328-38515-8

11 12 13 14 15 V010 19 18 17 16 15

Written by Tracy Sato
Illustrated by Ute Simon

Think about some of your favorite toys.
Children in the past played with cars molded
out of metal. They moved their cars by hand.

Now children can play with remote-controlled cars.

Construction sets have been a favorite of children for many years. One set had small wooden logs that could be stacked to make cabins and buildings.

Today construction kits have pieces that fit together and wheels or gears that allow movement. Sometimes motors are included to make machines that can move on their own.

Games like hopscotch have been popular for a long time.
Children would toss small rocks on a grid drawn in chalk.
Each player tried to hop in the squares without stumbling.

Boys and girls today play on playground equipment with many different activity areas. Some structures even have climbing walls and zip lines.

What were schools like long ago? Children of all ages sat next to each other on benches. They practiced lessons by repeating words out loud. That could be noisy!

In schools today, children can listen to stories at the listening center. They wear headphones so the noise doesn't bother anyone else. Other children can listen at the same time.

Then   Now

9

In the past, students exchanged letters with children at other schools. They were called pen pals. It was a fun way for children to learn about life in other places.

Today some classrooms have computers with webcams. These small cameras let children see each other on the computer monitor as they talk into a microphone. They can see and talk to someone miles away!

 Long ago children rode home from school in a buggy.
A horse pulled the buggy along a bumpy road.

Today children get home from school in many different ways. Some ride the bus, some ride in cars, and others walk.

People have been using telephones for many years. Early phones had no buttons or dials. An operator had to connect calls by plugging in different wires.

Now cell phones can be carried anywhere in a pocket or bag. No wires are needed. People can make calls from anywhere.

Home life was different in the past too. People once did their laundry by scrubbing wet clothes on washboards in large tubs. They would hang the clothes outside on clotheslines to dry.

Washers and dryers make doing laundry easier for families today. These machines also make the job go faster.

Then

Phonographs were a popular way to play music.
A large vinyl disk called a record was played by
setting a needle in its tiny grooves.

Music players have been transformed since the phonograph. Now you can use a computer to download songs to your personal music player. You can carry your favorite songs with you.

Newspapers have provided up-to-date information to people for many years. They may also tell about events and things to buy or sell, and include puzzles and comic strips.

While newspapers are still widely read, news can be accessed almost instantly from the Internet using a computer. News can be posted on the Internet minutes after it happens.

In many homes, families would gather around the radio in the living room after dinner. They would listen to adventure stories, funny skits, and mysteries.

Families may still gather after dinner today,
but now they watch television shows or movies.

As they did in the past, people today enjoy reading books. They can read books for fun and to learn new things.

Many things have changed, but some things will always stay the same.